Exploring visual arts

Easy-to-use, easy-to-follow art projects

by Agnes Russell

EXPLORING VISUAL ARTS
Ages 5–7

Published by
R.I.C. Publications® Pty Ltd
PO Box 332, Greenwood
Western Australia 6924

Published 2010

RIC–6582
ISBN–978-1-74126-845-4

Titles available in this series:
Exploring visual arts—Ages 5–7
Exploring visual arts—Ages 8–10
Exploring visual arts—Ages 11⁺

Distributed by:
UK/Republic of Ireland:
    Prim-Ed Publishing
    Bosheen
    New Ross
    County Wexford
    Republic of Ireland

USA:
    Didax Education
    395 Main Street
    Rowley
    MA 01969
    USA

Foreword

Exploring visual arts is a series of three books designed to provide teachers with a range of art lessons for a variety of age groups. Teaching visual arts can be challenging and rewarding. This series offers effective teaching strategies and activities providing skills, techniques and ideas that satisfy curriculum requirements with classroom-tested art projects.

Titles in this series include:

Exploring visual arts—Ages 5–7

Exploring visual arts—Ages 8–10

Exploring visual arts—Ages 11+

CONTENTS

Introduction

Being both a classroom teacher and an art specialist requires a lot of hard work and organisation. This is where an easy-to-use book, full of practical ideas comes in handy!

The activities in this series will provide teachers with a variety of art lessons based on different topics, suited to a range of age levels. Most art activities can be completed in one or two lessons, based on hourly lesson blocks.

At the back of the book is an easy-to-use assessment checklist as well as a student self-assessment sheet which can be adapted to any of the lessons in this book. Some timesaving hints have also been included to reduce preparation and clean-up time.

The lessons in this book give students the opportunity to create artworks through drawing, painting, collage and printmaking. The art activities have been used successfully with students from Years 1 to 7.

Happy art making!

Agnes Russell

CURRICULUM LINKS

WA	NSW	QLD	VIC.	SA
AI 2	VAS 1.1	VA 2.1	ARVA0201	1.1, 2.1
ASP 2	VAS 1.2	VA 2.2	ARPA0202	1.2, 2.2
AR 2	VAS 1.3	VA 2.3		1.3, 2.3
AIS 2	VAS 1.4			1.4, 2.4
				1.5, 2.5
				1.6, 2.6

R.I.C. Publications®

Timesaving tips

- Don't spend hours at the sink, washing out paint palettes at the end of the day, egg cartons make a perfect timesaving alternative to a paint palette as they don't require washing. Just close the lid when paint is no longer required. If the paint does dry up, only a quick refill is needed. Discourage students from mixing colours on the lid as it can glue the egg carton closed! When the egg cartons become worn out, just throw them away for recycling.

- Ice-cream container lids and styrofoam meat trays are perfect for colour mixing. A quick rinse makes them reusable.

- Large yoghurt containers make unbreakable water containers for rinsing brushes between colours. There is no broken glass to worry about if they are dropped!

- The school newsletter is a fantastic way of asking for donations of egg cartons and containers. You will be pleasantly surprised at what students bring.

- Have a good supply of scrap paper handy for early finishers. Raid the photocopy room for any photocopy errors. Students can draw on the back of these.

- Stencils and activity cards are a perfect way to occupy early finishers. They provide a little guidance to create some artwork without wasting paper with aimless scribbling. (Refer to pages 72–73 for some sample activity cards.) There is an endless number of ideas for art-related tasks which the students can complete.

- An art equipment trolley stacked with glue, scissors, lead pencils and erasers means students have initial equipment ready for beginning their art project and can organise themselves. This provides time to prepare any additional material that the students require.

- Have laminated pictures of famous artworks on hand. Art calendars and the internet are great resources for images.

- Always keep newspapers, some rags and spray cleaner handy for clean-up time. If students spread newspaper over their desks before an art lesson, it reduces the amount of mess on the desks.

- Step-by-step 'how to draw' books are a great way of teaching students by combining simple shapes to create an image. Some of the artworks in this book began with 'guided drawing'. Use a large sheet of lithograph or butcher's paper to demonstrate how to draw the object. Students then follow these instructions, one step at a time, to create their own drawing. This gives those students who are not very confident at drawing a boost as they can follow step-by-step instructions quite easily. It also provides the opportunity to discuss art elements such as line, shape etc.

Teachers notes

Each art project is explained over two pages:

- The teacher's instruction page includes information about the number of lessons required to complete the project, a list of materials, step-by-step instructions, evaluation suggestions for all art strands and, where applicable, variations of the project and drawing tips.

- A full-page colour photograph shows an example of the completed art project.

TEACHERS PAGE

Duration*: number of lessons required to complete the project is shown.

Task: explains what the student is required to do to complete each art project.

Lesson: gives step-by-step instructions for completing the art project.

Title: states the name of the art project

Materials: states what resources or equipment are required to complete the art project.

Evaluation: suggestions for each art strand are provided.

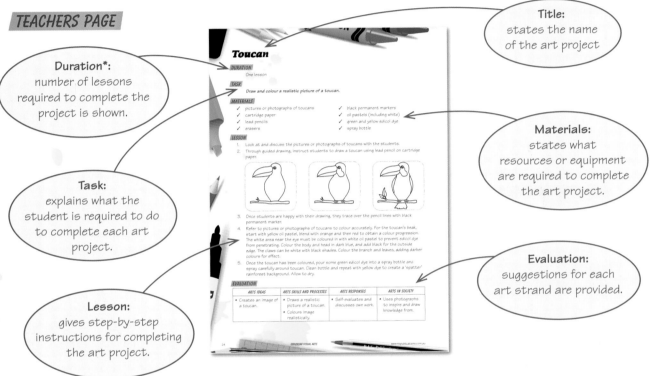

* Note: The suggested 'break-up' of lessons for projects which take more than one lesson may change depending on the need to allow painted work to dry, time constraints, the progress of the students and the availability of other work in the project which needs to be completed.

ART PROJECT PHOTOGRAPH

Title of the art project is stated.

A full-colour photograph* of the completed art project is provided.

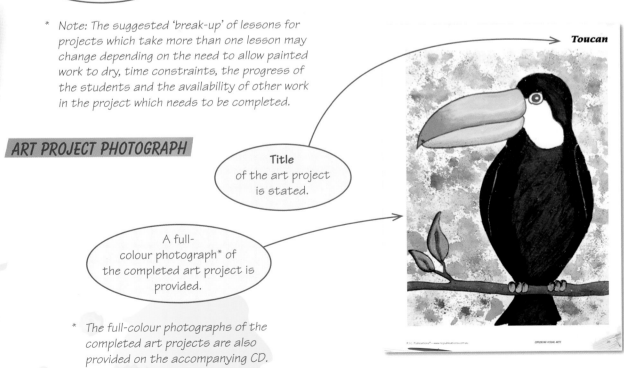

* The full-colour photographs of the completed art projects are also provided on the accompanying CD.

Teachers notes

- a **sample assessment checklist** on page 67, which can be used with any art project within the book and a **blank student assessment sheet** on page 68, which can be linked to an art project of the teacher's or student's choice

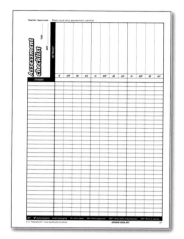

- resources which can be used as class stimulus posters including **'Looking at art'** sheet (page 69) and **'Elements of art'** labels (page 70)

- **reward ribbons** (page 71) to pin to students' artwork

- samples of **art activity cards** on pages 72 and 73 that can be used as 'early finisher' art activities, or relief teacher or extra homework activities

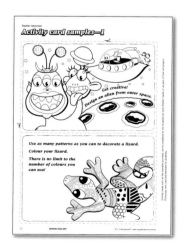
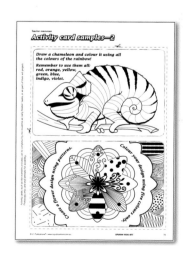

- **templates** on pages 74–76 to accompany particular art projects.

Striped chameleon

DURATION
Two lessons

TASK
Draw a picture of a chameleon and colour using different shades of green.

MATERIALS

- ✓ photographs and scientific pictures of chameleons
- ✓ lead pencils
- ✓ cartridge paper
- ✓ black permanent markers

- ✓ water-soluble crayons
- ✓ water and containers
- ✓ paintbrushes
- ✓ scissors

- ✓ googly eyes
- ✓ PVA glue
- ✓ green pipe-cleaners
- ✓ green card

LESSON 1

1. Look at scientific pictures and photographs of chameleons and discuss the features.
2. On the cartridge paper, use the pencil to sketch a picture of a chameleon sitting on a branch. Include the features previously discussed.
3. Draw stripes on the chameleon's body.
4. Trace over the pencil lines with black permanent marker.
5. Look at the various tones of green available in the crayon selection (light, medium, dark). Choose two shades of green and colour the chameleon, alternating the colour for each stripe.
6. Colour the tree branch, using brown crayon.
7. Paint over crayon using water and brush, dissolving the crayon to create a paint effect. Allow to dry.

LESSON 2

Cut out chameleon and branch. Glue onto green card. Use PVA glue to attach the googly eye and curled pipe-cleaner for tongue.

EVALUATION

ARTS IDEAS	ARTS SKILLS AND PROCESSES	ARTS RESPONSES	ARTS IN SOCIETY
• Makes a drawing of a chameleon using lines and shapes.	• Matches and groups similar colours. • Uses simple terminology such as light and dark to describe colours.	• Responds to visual art—e.g. photographs—by making another artwork.	• Looks at scientific artwork from magazines.

VARIATIONS

1. Draw a chameleon on diffusing* paper and colour with felt-tip pen. Spray with water to diffuse colours.

    * Diffusing paper is available from art/craft supply shops in packs of 50.

2. Cut and paste different coloured scraps of paper to create a leafy background.

The cat sat on the mat

DURATION

Two lessons

TASK

1. **To draw a cat then create a collage of different shades of orange tissue paper to represent the texture and tone of a cat's fur.**
2. **To paint a decorative mat for the cat collage.**

MATERIALS

- ✓ photographs or pictures of rug designs from Mexico
- ✓ 2 sheets of cartridge paper
- ✓ lead pencils
- ✓ black permanent markers
- ✓ paint in various bright colours

- ✓ glue
- ✓ tissue paper in different shades of orange
- ✓ paintbrushes
- ✓ water and containers
- ✓ scissors

LESSON 1

1. Look at examples of Mexican rug designs. Discuss the colours and patterns used. Students use these ideas to draw their own rug design on cartridge paper using lead pencil.
2. Trace over the rug design with black permanent marker.
3. Paint rug design using bold, bright colours. Allow to dry.

LESSON 2

1. On second sheet of paper, students use pencil to draw cat either sitting or lying down, including features such as eyes, nose, whiskers etc. Trace over the lines in black permanent marker.
2. Tear orange tissue paper into small shapes, approximately the size of a bottle top.
3. Glue torn tissue paper pieces on top of the cat, overlapping shapes and colours. When dry, retrace marker lines if necessary.
4. Cut out and glue onto painted mat.

EVALUATION

ARTS IDEAS	ARTS SKILLS AND PROCESSES	ARTS RESPONSES	ARTS IN SOCIETY
• Makes a drawing of a decorative rug using a variety of shapes and patterns.	• Uses tissue paper to create tone or texture on a collage. • Paints a simple pattern design.	• Responds to visual art through making another artwork (e.g. looks at photographs to aid drawing).	• Looks at Mexican textile designs and discusses pattern and colour use.

EXPLORING VISUAL ARTS

R.I.C. Publications®

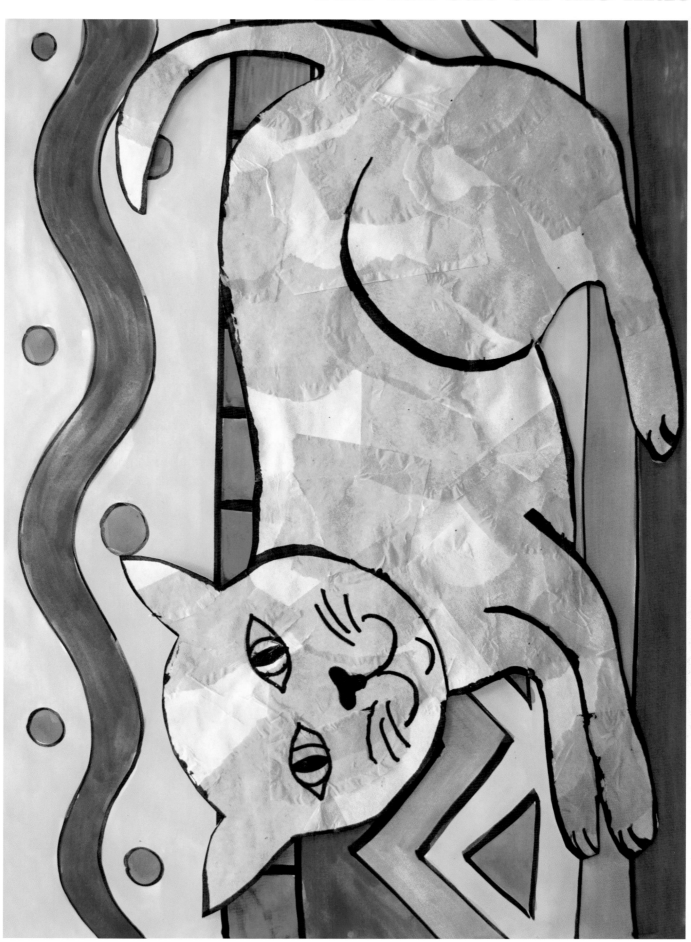

Waterlilies

DURATION

One lesson

TASK

Look at the shape and form of waterlilies then draw one and colour using only cool colours.

MATERIALS

✓ photographs or pictures of waterlilies
✓ lead pencils
✓ dark blue or purple card cut into long lengths
✓ oil pastels
✓ white crayon

LESSON

1. Look at pictures of waterlilies. Discuss the shape of the lily pad, the way the petals of the flower are pointy and overlap each other, the different tones of petals, the lines on the lily pad etc.
2. Students lightly sketch the waterlily on dark blue card, capturing the shape of the flower, the long stem and the lily pad. Smaller lilies can be drawn in the background if desired.
3. Colour the waterlily and pad using various shades of purple and green oil pastels. White crayon can be used to highlight areas on the petals and stem as well as creating water ripple lines in the background.

EVALUATION

ARTS IDEAS	ARTS SKILLS AND PROCESSES	ARTS RESPONSES	ARTS IN SOCIETY
• Combines elements of line, shape and colour to create realistic interpretations of waterlilies.	• Matches similar shades of various colours. • Colour using an oil pastel medium.	• Responds to visual arts through making another artwork (e.g. looks at photographs to aid drawings).	• Looks at photographs and botanical pictures.

R.I.C. Publications®

Sunflower

DURATION

Three lessons

TASK

Create a collage of a sunflower.

MATERIALS

- ✓ pictures or photographs of sunflowers
- ✓ 3 shades of yellow paint (see Lesson 1 below)
- ✓ 3 x A4 sheets of cartridge paper
- ✓ black and brown crepe paper pieces
- ✓ lead pencils
- ✓ glue
- ✓ scissors
- ✓ green oil pastels
- ✓ blue card
- ✓ brushes
- ✓ water and containers

LESSON 1

1. Show the students pictures of sunflowers. Discuss the colours and shapes.

2. Mix three different shades of yellow. (*Yellow + white to create pale yellow; bright yellow directly from the container; yellow + brown to create ochre.*) Instruct the students to paint three sheets of cartridge paper using the different shades of yellow. Allow to dry. (*Alternatively, different shades of yellow origami paper may be used for the petals.*)

LESSON 2

1. Students draw a large circle in lead pencil for the sunflower face and a smaller circle inside it on the top half of the blue card. Draw the sunflower stem and leaves using green oil pastels. Use darker shades of green to highlight areas on the stem and leaves.

2. Scrunch crepe paper pieces to glue onto the sunflower face—black in the centre circle and brown around the outside. Allow to dry.

LESSON 3

1. Draw petal shapes on the three different sheets of yellow paper and cut out.

2. Glue the petals around the sunflower face, overlapping and varying colours.

EVALUATION

ARTS IDEAS	ARTS SKILLS AND PROCESSES	ARTS RESPONSES	ARTS IN SOCIETY
• Draws various flower parts onto a selection of collage materials.	• Uses a variety of materials to make a collage of an image.	• Responds to visual arts (e.g. Van Gogh's sunflower paintings) by making another artwork.	• Looks at Van Gogh's sunflower paintings and discusses the various shades of yellow used.

EXPLORING VISUAL ARTS

R.I.C. Publications®

EXPLORING VISUAL ARTS

Monet's waterlilies

DURATION

Two lessons

TASK

Draw and paint a waterlily garden scene based on Claude Monet's famous waterlily paintings.

MATERIALS

- ✓ pictures or photographs of Monet's waterlilies—Givenchy, France
- ✓ dark blue and light blue card
- ✓ paint in various colours
- ✓ brushes
- ✓ water and containers
- ✓ oil pastels (including white)
- ✓ scissors
- ✓ glue

LESSON 1

1. Look at Claude Monet's artwork featuring his paintings of waterlilies and garden bridge. Discuss his painting techniques (short brushstrokes, dabbles and splashes of colour, catching light and reflections in his work etc.).

2. On the light blue card, students use white oil pastels or paint to draw a garden bridge. Below the bridge, dab on various colours of paint using paintbrush or fingers. Encourage students to mix and overlap colours to create the impression of reflection on water. Allow to dry.

LESSON 2

1. Students use white oil pastel to draw simple waterlily shapes. Outline in pink or purple to give more definition.

2. At the bottom of each flower, students draw a lily pad and colour in shades of green.

3. Cut out the bridge along the top curve. Assist students in cutting out the middle areas of the bridge. Glue onto dark blue card.

EVALUATION

ARTS IDEAS	ARTS SKILLS AND PROCESSES	ARTS RESPONSES	ARTS IN SOCIETY
• Creates an artwork inspired by the art of others, exploring style.	• Paints using a range of colours and applicators to achieve a specific effect.	• Responds to the visual art of others. (e.g. Monet's waterlily paintings)	• Discusses the art or life of Claude Monet and realises that some artists earn a living from their artwork.

Self-portrait with striped background

DURATION

Two lessons

TASK

Draw and colour a self-portrait.

MATERIALS

- ✓ cartridge paper
- ✓ mirrors
- ✓ lead pencils
- ✓ erasers
- ✓ black permanent markers
- ✓ oil pastels
- ✓ ruler

LESSON 1

1. Students look in the mirror to observe their own facial features. Discuss the correct positioning of eyes, ears etc.
2. Using cartridge paper and lead pencil, instruct students to draw their self-portrait, using the mirror as an aid. Refer to *Tips for drawing: Faces*, if necessary.
3. Trace over portrait in black permanent marker and colour using oil pastels. Blend and mix colours to create a skin effect and shadowed areas of face.

LESSON 2

Use a ruler to create a striped background. Choose two different colours to fill in the stripes.

EVALUATION

ARTS IDEAS	ARTS SKILLS AND PROCESSES	ARTS RESPONSES	ARTS IN SOCIETY
• Draws a realistic self-portrait.	• Draws a self-portrait using correct positioning of facial features. • Shades self-portrait using realistic colours.	• Self-evaluates and discusses own work.	• Looks at the importance of portraiture through time before the invention of cameras.

TIPS FOR DRAWING: FACES

Start with an oval shape. Add a faint vertical line to use as a guide for the nose and another line horizontally across the middle as a guide for the eyes. Eyes are positioned an eye width apart. The nose is as wide as the gap between the eyes and halfway between the eyes and chin. The ends of the lips line up with the pupils in the eyes. The ears are level with the eyebrows and the bottom of the nose.

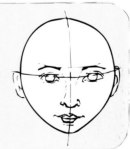

Self-portrait with striped background

Painted self-portrait

DURATION

One lesson

TASK

Paint a self-portrait.

MATERIALS

- ✓ mirrors
- ✓ lead pencils
- ✓ erasers
- ✓ black permanent markers
- ✓ paint and brushes
- ✓ cartridge paper
- ✓ water and containers

LESSON

1. Students look in the mirror to observe their own facial features. Discuss the correct positioning of eyes, ears etc. Refer to *Tips for drawing: Faces*, if necessary.
2. Using cartridge paper and lead pencil, instruct students to draw their portrait, using the mirror as an aid.
3. Trace over the pencil drawing with black permanent marker.
4. Paint the self-portrait using realistic colours. Mix the colours to create light and dark areas on the face, hair etc. Ensure students wash brushes thoroughly between colours.
5. Paint the background using either one block colour or a pattern of colours.

EVALUATION

ARTS IDEAS	ARTS SKILLS AND PROCESSES	ARTS RESPONSES	ARTS IN SOCIETY
• Draws a realistic self-portrait.	• Draws a self-portrait using correct positioning of facial features. • Paints self-portrait using appropriate colours.	• Self-evaluates and discusses own work.	• Looks at the importance of portraiture through time before the invention of cameras.

TIPS FOR DRAWING: FACES

Start with an oval shape. Add a faint vertical line to use as a guide for the nose and another line horizontally across the middle as a guide for the eyes. Eyes are positioned an eye width apart. The nose is as wide as the gap between the eyes and halfway between the eyes and chin. The ends of the lips line up with the pupils in the eyes. The ears are level with the eyebrows and the bottom of the nose.

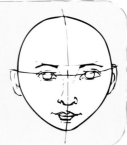

R.I.C. Publications®

Painted self-portrait

Starry night

DURATION

One lesson

TASK

Create an interpretation of Van Gogh's 'Starry night' painting, using chalk pastels.

MATERIALS

- ✓ a copy of Van Gogh's 'Starry night' from a book or internet source
- ✓ dark blue card
- ✓ chalk pastels
- ✓ spray fixative

LESSON

1. Look at Van Gogh's 'Starry night' painting. Discuss the content of the painting (swirling clouds, stars with exaggerated features, movement in the sky, curves or dots for stars, dark rolling hills of the horizon etc.). Discuss the colours and the painting technique.

2. On dark blue card, students draw their own interpretation of 'Starry night' in chalk pastels, using short strokes to create the swirling effect in the night sky.

3. Spray with fixative to prevent smudging.

EVALUATION

ARTS IDEAS	ARTS SKILLS AND PROCESSES	ARTS RESPONSES	ARTS IN SOCIETY
• Uses ideas of other artists to inspire own work.	• Uses chalk pastels effectively to create a specific effect.	• Responds to visual arts by making another artwork.	• Looks at Van Gogh's 'Starry night' and other works and discusses painting techniques.

R.I.C. Publications®

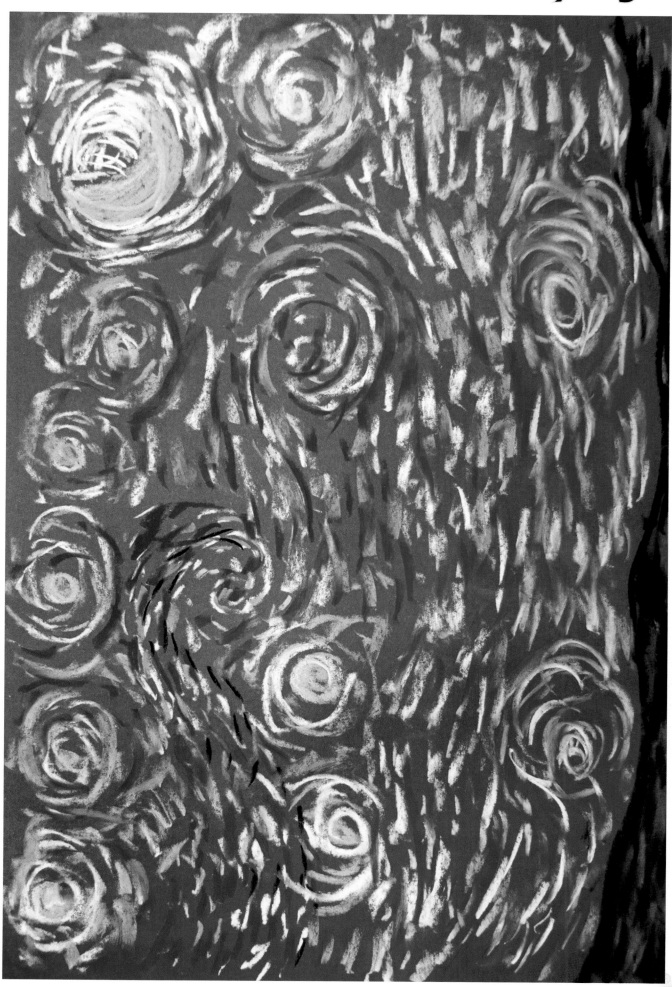

Farm cow

DURATION

Two lessons

TASK

Create a collage of a dairy cow.

MATERIALS

- ✓ coloured pictures or photographs of barns and cows
- ✓ green card
- ✓ white cartridge paper
- ✓ red and black origami paper
- ✓ scissors
- ✓ glue
- ✓ scrap paper
- ✓ black permanent markers
- ✓ lead pencils
- ✓ erasers
- ✓ pink coloured pencils

LESSON 1

1. Look at and discuss the pictures of barns. What shape is the roof? How many doors and windows are there? Why is the barn door wide and tall?

2. Create a farm background on green card by drawing a barn on the red origami paper. Cut out and glue on left or right side of the green paper. Cut door and window shapes from black origami paper and glue onto barn.

3. Cut long strips of white paper to make a fence. Glue next to the barn.

LESSON 2

1. Look at and discuss the pictures of cows. What colours can dairy cows be? What shape is the head, ears and body? How many legs? What shape are the hooves? What does the end of the tail look like?

2. Practice drawing a cow on scrap paper.

3. On cartridge paper, draw a dairy cow using lead pencil. Trace in black permanent marker. Draw and colour patches on the cow's body using black permanent marker.

4. Use pink pencil to colour the cow's nose and udder.

5. Cut out cow and glue in foreground of picture. (Some part may cover the barn and fence.)

EVALUATION

ARTS IDEAS	ARTS SKILLS AND PROCESSES	ARTS RESPONSES	ARTS IN SOCIETY
• Generates ideas for creating images based on a theme.	• Creates an image using drawing and collage.	• Self-evaluates and discusses own work.	• Expresses thoughts and feelings through art making.

Rooster

DURATION

Two lessons

TASK

Create a collage of a rooster.

MATERIALS

- ✓ pictures or photographs of roosters
- ✓ orange or yellow card
- ✓ brown origami paper
- ✓ lead pencils
- ✓ scissors
- ✓ glue

- ✓ black permanent markers
- ✓ cartridge paper
- ✓ oil pastels
- ✓ wooden skewer
- ✓ PVA glue (optional if using feathers)
- ✓ coloured feathers (optional)

LESSON 1

1. On orange or yellow card, create a farm background in the following way: Draw a small farmhouse silhouette on brown origami paper. Cut out and glue onto card about one-third of the way down the page. Use black permanent marker to draw a fence next to the farmhouse.

2. Cut a long strip of brown origami paper into smaller sections and glue along the bottom of the page to create a picket fence effect.

LESSON 2

1. Look at and discuss the pictures or photographs of roosters. Discuss the shapes, sizes and colours of body parts.

2. On cartridge paper, draw a large rooster using lead pencil. Trace over the rooster with a black permanent marker and colour using two or three different coloured oil pastels.

3. To create a textured feather effect, gently scratch lines into the rooster's body using a skewer.

4. Cut out the rooster and glue onto the coloured card to make it look like the rooster is standing on the picket fence.

5. Glue coloured feathers onto the tail using PVA glue, if desired.

EVALUATION

ARTS IDEAS	ARTS SKILLS AND PROCESSES	ARTS RESPONSES	ARTS IN SOCIETY
• Generates ideas for creating images based on a theme.	• Creates an image using drawing and collage.	• Self-evaluates and discusses own artwork.	• Expresses thoughts and feelings through art making.

Hessian elephant

DURATION

Two lessons

TASK

Create a collage of an elephant using hessian and various types of paper.

MATERIALS

- ✓ pictures or photographs of elephants
- ✓ hessian squares
- ✓ grey and white paint
- ✓ brushes
- ✓ water and containers
- ✓ scissors
- ✓ PVA glue
- ✓ black wool

- ✓ brown crepe paper
- ✓ green cupcake papers
- ✓ brown oil pastels
- ✓ green card
- ✓ green oil pastels (optional)
- ✓ googly eyes
- ✓ small pieces of grey card

LESSON 1

1. Based on pictures and class discussions about elephants, students paint a side view of an elephant onto hessian, using grey paint. Add tusks in white paint. Allow to dry while preparing background.

LESSON 2

1. Place the green card on a rough surface such as a concrete path. Rub the side of a brown oil pastel along the bottom third of the green card. This will create a 'rocky ground' effect.

2. Tear brown crepe paper into small pieces, scrunch and glue to make trunks for palm trees.

3. Cut two cupcake papers into quarters. Cut along rippled edges to make palm fronds. Glue three cupcake quarters to the top of each trunk. Add extra 'jungle' plants if desired by drawing with green oil pastel.

4. Cut around outside edge of hessian elephant. Use PVA glue to attach the elephant to the background. Glue on googly eye and small length of black wool for the tail. Cut an ear shape from grey card, fold the short edge under and glue onto correct area of elephant's body. (Do not glue the ear down flat. Allow the larger edge to stand out from the body to create a better 3D-effect.)

EVALUATION

ARTS IDEAS	ARTS SKILLS AND PROCESSES	ARTS RESPONSES	ARTS IN SOCIETY
• Creates an image of an elephant.	• Uses collage materials effectively.	• Self-evaluates and discusses own work.	• Expresses thoughts and feelings through art making.

R.I.C. Publications®

Toucan

DURATION

One lesson

TASK

Draw and colour a realistic picture of a toucan.

MATERIALS

- ✓ pictures or photographs of toucans
- ✓ cartridge paper
- ✓ lead pencils
- ✓ erasers

- ✓ black permanent markers
- ✓ oil pastels (including white)
- ✓ green and yellow edicol dye
- ✓ spray bottle

LESSON

1. Look at and discuss the pictures or photographs of toucans with the students.

2. Through guided drawing, instruct students to draw a toucan using lead pencil on cartridge paper.

3. Once students are happy with their drawing, they trace over the pencil lines with black permanent marker.

4. Refer to pictures or photographs of toucans to colour accurately. For the toucan's beak, start with yellow oil pastel, blend with orange and then red to obtain a colour progression. The white area near the eye must be coloured in with white oil pastel to prevent edicol dye from penetrating. Colour the body and head in dark blue, and add black for the outside edge. The claws can be white with black shades. Colour the branch and leaves, adding darker colours for effect.

5. Once the toucan has been coloured, pour some green edicol dye into a spray bottle and spray carefully around toucan. Clean bottle and repeat with yellow dye to create a 'spatter' rainforest background. Allow to dry.

EVALUATION

ARTS IDEAS	ARTS SKILLS AND PROCESSES	ARTS RESPONSES	ARTS IN SOCIETY
• Creates an image of a toucan.	• Draws a realistic picture of a toucan. • Colours image realistically.	• Self-evaluates and discusses own work.	• Uses photographs to inspire and draw knowledge from.

Wool snail

DURATION

Three lessons

TASK

Create a picture of a snail using drawing and various materials.

MATERIALS

- ✓ light and dark green card
- ✓ thick card
- ✓ grey card
- ✓ lead pencils

- ✓ black permanent marker
- ✓ small googly eyes
- ✓ PVA glue

- ✓ scissors
- ✓ wool in a variety of colours
- ✓ matches (optional)

LESSON 1

Through guided drawing, the students draw a simple snail shell using lead pencil on thick card and, on grey card, the body, head and eyestalks. Trace over the lines using black permanent marker. Cut out both pieces.

thick card

grey card

LESSON 2

1. Cut wool in approximately 30 cm lengths. Glue close together on snail shell in a swirling pattern, so that very little thick card shows through.

2. When snail shell is completed, glue the grey body, then the shell onto dark green card. Attach eyes to eyestalks.

LESSON 3

Use light green card and black permanent markers to draw and the cut out a variety of leaf shapes. Glue these around the snail, but if time and resources permit, carefully burn the edges of the leaves to create more natural and interesting leaf shapes. A similar effect may also be created by tracing around the edge of the shape of the leaves in brown crayon or pastel before cutting and gluing.

EVALUATION

ARTS IDEAS	ARTS SKILLS AND PROCESSES	ARTS RESPONSES	ARTS IN SOCIETY
• Generates ideas for creating images based on a theme.	• Uses a variety of materials to create a specific effect on a collage.	• Self-evaluates and discusses own work.	• Expresses thoughts and feelings through art making.

African animal patterns

DURATION

Two lessons

TASK

Create a paper collage based on selected African animal patterns.

MATERIALS

- ✓ photographs or pictures of tigers, zebras, leopards, giraffes etc.
- ✓ glue
- ✓ scissors
- ✓ black card (large)

- ✓ orange, yellow, white card (small)
- ✓ black tissue paper
- ✓ black origami paper
- ✓ brown origami paper

LESSON 1

1. Look at the photographs or pictures of tigers, zebras, leopards and giraffes and discuss the patterns on the fur.

2. Tear strips of black tissue paper to resemble tiger stripes (thick in the middle, pointed and thin at the ends). Glue onto orange card.

3. Cut long strips of black paper (make sure they have a slight bend) and glue onto white card to make zebra prints.

LESSON 2

1. Tear black paper into disc shapes and glue onto the yellow card. Tear smaller disc shapes from the brown paper and glue onto the middle of the black discs for a leopard pattern.

2. Arrange all three animal patterns on a large sheet of black card. Cut the patterns to shape and glue them, arranged in an interesting way.

EVALUATION

ARTS IDEAS	ARTS SKILLS AND PROCESSES	ARTS RESPONSES	ARTS IN SOCIETY
• Generates ideas for creating images based on a theme.	• Arranges paper to create a specific effect on a collage.	• Self-evaluates and discusses own work.	• Expresses thoughts and feelings through art making.

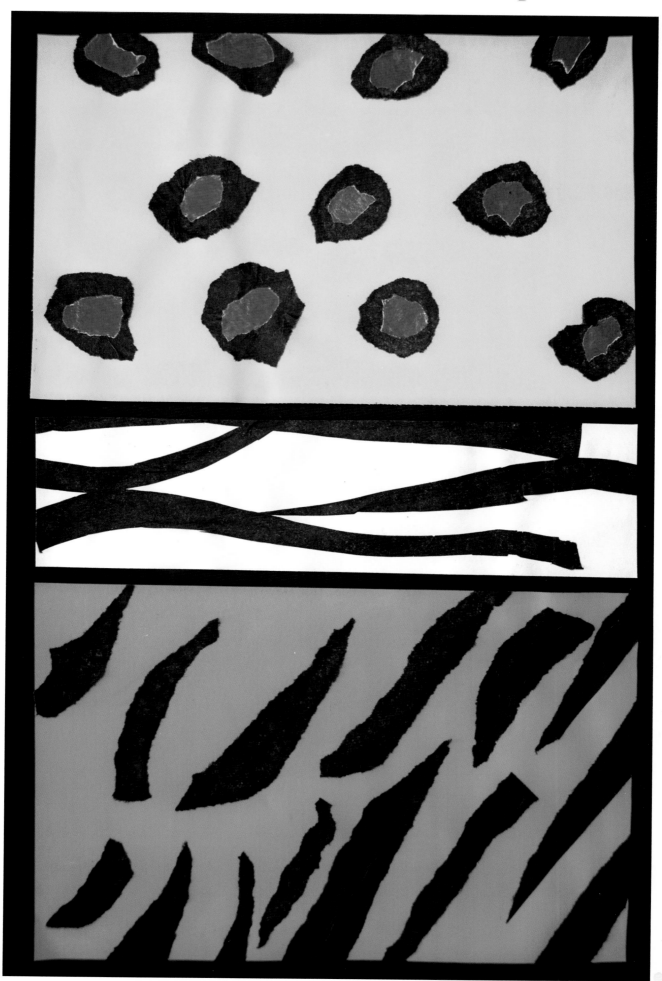

Build-a-dinosaur

DURATION

Two lessons

TASK

Create a dinosaur image from a variety of geometric shapes.

MATERIALS

✓ build-a-dinosaur template (see page 74)
✓ watercolour pencils (if not available, normal coloured pencils or markers will do)
✓ dinosaur pictures (optional)
✓ brushes

✓ water and containers
✓ scissors
✓ green card
✓ glue

LESSON 1

Provide each child with a copy of the geometric shapes template (on page 74). The students will need to colour each shape using watercolour pencils. Once all shapes have been coloured, paint over the shapes with water to dissolve the pencil pigment. Leave to dry.

LESSON 2

1. Once shapes are dry, the students carefully cut them out.

2. On green card, the students arrange the shapes to make a dinosaur. (Some dinosaur pictures may be useful at this point to help students compile an image.)

3. Once the students are happy with their arrangement, they carefully glue down their shapes, one at a time, so they do not rearrange their image.

EVALUATION

ARTS IDEAS	ARTS SKILLS AND PROCESSES	ARTS RESPONSES	ARTS IN SOCIETY
• Generates ideas for creating a dinosaur image using various shapes.	• Carefully cuts out shapes. • Uses watercolour pencils effectively. • Uses shapes to create a collage of an image.	• Self-evaluates and discusses own work.	• Expresses thoughts and feelings through art making.

VARIATIONS

1. Print sponge shapes, using different colours of paint, onto cartridge paper. Allow to dry, cut out and rearrange into a dinosaur. Trace the edges with black permanent marker.

2. Use the sides of thick cardboard pieces to print a 'prehistoric' background for the shape. Use only one or two colours for the dinosaur so that the dinosaur image is not too 'busy'.

Striped tiger

DURATION

DURATION

One lesson

TASK

Draw a tiger and use black paper strips to create the pattern of the tiger's fur.

MATERIALS

- ✓ orange and green card
- ✓ lead pencils
- ✓ erasers
- ✓ black permanent marker
- ✓ PVA glue
- ✓ googly eyes
- ✓ black origami paper
- ✓ scissors
- ✓ glue

LESSON

1. Use guided drawing to enable the students to draw a tiger on the orange card.

2. When the students are happy with their drawing, trace over it with black permanent marker. Colour the nose and insides of the ears black.

3. Cut tiger stripes from black paper, making sure the ends come to a fine point.

4. Arrange stripes on the tiger's face, back, belly, tail and legs. Cut to fit and glue in place.

5. Cut tiger out and glue onto green card. Attach googly eyes using PVA glue.

EVALUATION

ARTS IDEAS	ARTS SKILLS AND PROCESSES	ARTS RESPONSES	ARTS IN SOCIETY
• Generates ideas for creating images based on a theme.	• Follows step-by-step instructions for drawing an image. • Cuts and glues paper to create specific effect on a collage.	• Self-evaluates and discusses own work.	• Expresses thoughts and feelings through art making.

Line portrait

DURATION

Two lessons

TASK

Create a self-portrait using only line to enhance detail and pattern.

MATERIALS

- ✓ cartridge paper
- ✓ lead pencils
- ✓ erasers
- ✓ fine black markers
- ✓ black permanent markers

LESSON 1

1. Explain to the students that they are going to draw a self-portrait of their whole body. Before the students begin, use one student as a 'model' to explain the body proportions that the students will need to think about when they are drawing themselves. Refer to *Tips for drawing: The human body* below.

2. The students use lead pencil to lightly draw the basic proportions. Once they are happy with all the shapes and sizes, trace over the lines in black permanent marker.

3. Fine black marker can be used to add detail and pattern to clothing, hair etc.

LESSON 2

1. Draw a background such as a place they enjoy spending time in.

2. Remind the students that they can only use *line* to add pattern or shading.

3. Because these pictures are quite simple in regards to colour, they look more effective mounted on brightly coloured card. Black card also works well.

EVALUATION

ARTS IDEAS	ARTS SKILLS AND PROCESSES	ARTS RESPONSES	ARTS IN SOCIETY
• Generates ideas for creating a self-portrait.	• Draws self using correct body proportions. • Uses line to create pattern and shading.	• Self-evaluates and discusses own work.	• Looks at the importance of portraiture through time.

TIPS FOR DRAWING: THE HUMAN BODY

The head can be used as a unit of measure to divide the body into six equal parts. The students can divide their page into six parts either by folding or drawing very faint lines across the page.

The six parts are, approximately: the head; the neck to just above the elbows; just above elbows to the waist; the waist to the middle of the thigh; the middle of the thigh to below the knee (the knees should be in the middle of this section), below the knee to the feet.

R.I.C. Publications®

Ladybug/Ladybird print

DURATION

Two lessons

TASK

Create a print of a ladybug/ladybird and a collage of a garden background.

MATERIALS

- ✓ red card
- ✓ black paint
- ✓ roller
- ✓ square of bubble wrap
- ✓ black permanent markers
- ✓ lead pencils
- ✓ googly eyes
- ✓ PVA glue
- ✓ scissors
- ✓ coloured origami paper
- ✓ green card

LESSON 1

1. Roll black paint over bubble wrap. Place a sheet of red card onto bubble wrap and gently smooth over with hands.
2. Peel card carefully from bubble wrap and leave to dry.
3. While print is drying, prepare background. Cut flower and leaf shapes from coloured origami paper and glue onto green card. Leave some space in the centre for the ladybug/ladybird. Allow to dry.

LESSON 2

1. Draw a large oval shape on the dry bubble print for the ladybug/ladybird's body and cut out.
2. Use black permanent marker to colour the top section of the ladybug/ladybird's body to create the head. Glue on googly eyes.
3. Glue ladybug/ladybird onto background. Use black permanent marker to draw legs and antennae.

EVALUATION

ARTS IDEAS	ARTS SKILLS AND PROCESSES	ARTS RESPONSES	ARTS IN SOCIETY
• Generates ideas for an artwork.	• Makes a print. • Creates a collage using paper to create an image.	• Self-evaluates and discusses own work	• Discusses the various forms of printmaking and their uses.

VARIATIONS

String print

1. Draw a ladybug/ladybird picture on thick card.
2. Put PVA glue on lines. Glue string on top of pencil lines.
3. When dry, roll black paint over entire picture. Press a sheet of red paper on top to make a print.

R.I.C. Publications®

Me and my clothes

DURATION

Two lessons

TASK

Create a collage of a human figure with paper clothes.

MATERIALS

✓ person template (see page 75)
✓ skin-coloured paper/paint
✓ lead pencils
✓ glue
✓ scissors

✓ coloured origami paper
✓ coloured card for background and ground
✓ hair-coloured wool (eg. black, brown, yellow, orange, red)
✓ fine coloured markers or pens

LESSON 1

1. Trace or photocopy the person template from page 75 onto skin-coloured paper for the students. Alternatively, the person template can be photocopied onto white paper and then painted in a skin colour.

2. The students will need to carefully cut out the template. Place coloured origami paper underneath the template to trace around the body shape to make paper clothes. Demonstrate for the students so they will know where to add sleeves etc.

3. Once the clothes have been drawn, cut out and glue onto the person. The students can overlap the clothes and create patterns on the clothes, shoes, belts etc.

LESSON 2

1. Glue wool pieces on the head for hair and add a hat if desired.

2. On coloured background card, attach a strip of contrasting coloured card along the bottom for the ground.

3. Glue the person onto the coloured card and add facial features using fine coloured markers.

EVALUATION

ARTS IDEAS	ARTS SKILLS AND PROCESSES	ARTS RESPONSES	ARTS IN SOCIETY
• Generates ideas to create a clothed person collage.	• Cuts out carefully. • Traces and cuts shapes to match template.	• Self-evaluates and discusses own work.	• Expresses thoughts and feelings through art making.

R.I.C. Publications®

Aboriginal hand art

DURATION

DURATION

One lesson

TASK

Create artwork based on Aboriginal art.

MATERIALS

- ✓ pictures, photographs or examples of Aboriginal art
- ✓ cartridge paper
- ✓ oil pastels

- ✓ lead pencils
- ✓ card for hand outline
- ✓ black edicol dye
- ✓ spray bottle

LESSON

1. Look at and discuss examples of Australian Aboriginal art. Pay particular attention to colour and pattern.
2. The students trace around their hand using pencil on card and cut out the shape.
3. Use brown, black, yellow and white oil pastel to make a concentric dot pattern on the cartridge paper.
4. When dot pattern is complete, put the hand shape in the middle of the cartridge paper and spray with black edicol dye. (Take care when spraying around the hand so dye does not get under the hand shape.)
5. When the edicol dye is dry, carefully remove the hand card to reveal a white hand shape.

Caution: In some areas it may be considered culturally inappropriate for non-Aboriginal people to create dot art pictures.

EVALUATION

ARTS IDEAS	ARTS SKILLS AND PROCESSES	ARTS RESPONSES	ARTS IN SOCIETY
• Generates ideas to create artworks based on a particular theme.	• Creates a concentric dot pattern.	• Responds to visual art through making another artwork.	• Looks at examples of Aboriginal artworks and discusses processes and techniques used.

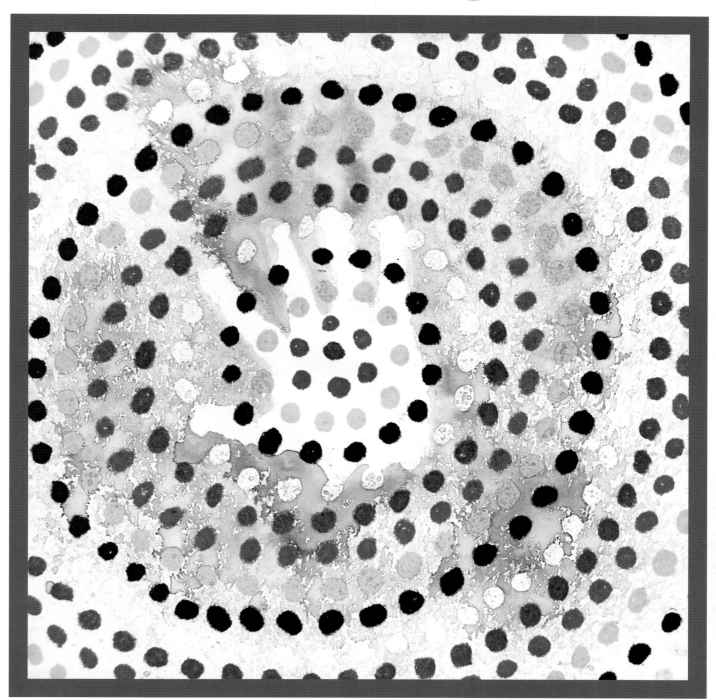

Lighthouse

DURATION
Two lessons

TASK

Draw and colour a lighthouse on a rocky shore; paint a selected background depicting various times of day and weather conditions.

MATERIALS

- ✓ 2 sheets of cartridge paper
- ✓ paint
- ✓ brushes
- ✓ water and containers
- ✓ black permanent marker

- ✓ lead pencils
- ✓ erasers
- ✓ oil pastels
- ✓ scissors
- ✓ glue

LESSON 1

1. Discuss the main features of a lighthouse with the students and model drawing one. Include a discussion of the location to introduce the rocky shore.

2. Students then draw their own lighthouse and shore on one sheet of cartridge paper using lead pencil. Once students are happy with their drawing, they trace over it with black permanent marker.

3. Use oil pastels to colour the lighthouse. To give the rocky shore a three-dimensional effect, students colour the rocks, starting at the base with dark brown then light brown and grey, blending colours gradually. Each rock needs to be coloured individually, so they need to be drawn quite large.

LESSON 2

1. Students can select which background they would like to paint—sunset (strips of blue, red, orange and yellow paint, slightly blended); night-time (purple blending into dark blue and black. Once dry, a moon can be drawn in white oil pastel or a circle of foil paper glued on); stormy (sponge paint grey and white); day-time (paint paper in bright blue, spread blobs of white paint to give impression of streaks of cloud).

2. When background is dry, students cut out lighthouse and rocky shore and glue onto background, taking care to align the bottom edge of the paper.

EVALUATION

ARTS IDEAS	ARTS SKILLS AND PROCESSES	ARTS RESPONSES	ARTS IN SOCIETY
• Generates ideas for creating images based on a theme (e.g. lighthouses).	• Draws using a variety of tools and media. • Paints to create specific effects.	• Self-evaluates and discusses own artwork.	• Expresses thoughts and feelings through art making (e.g. choosing background for lighthouse).

R.I.C. Publications®

Under the sea

Two lessons

TASK

Paint an underwater scene.

MATERIALS

- ✓ cartridge paper (one full and one half sheet)
- ✓ lead pencils
- ✓ erasers
- ✓ blue, green, red, yellow, orange paint
- ✓ cotton buds
- ✓ brushes
- ✓ water and containers
- ✓ scrap origami paper
- ✓ PVA glue
- ✓ small googly eyes
- ✓ scissors
- ✓ black permanent markers

LESSON 1

1. Draw coral shapes on the full sheet of cartridge paper. Trace over them in black permanent marker.
2. Paint around the coral shapes in blue paint, covering the background.
3. Dip the cotton buds into coloured paint and carefully make dot patterns inside the coral shapes. Set aside to dry.
4. On the half sheet of cartridge paper, paint a seahorse shape using fingers and knuckles and orange paper. Demonstrate first to ensure that the students are able to use their hands correctly to create an image which resembles a seahorse. Allow to dry.

LESSON 2

1. Cut out the seahorse and glue onto the coral reef background. Do not glue the head down completetly as the frilly coronet must be inserted beneath.
2. Scraps of origami paper can be used to create fins, the coronet or spots on the seahorse if they were not included when painted.
3. Use PVA glue to attach a googly eye to the seahorse.

EVALUATION

ARTS IDEAS	ARTS SKILLS AND PROCESSES	ARTS RESPONSES	ARTS IN SOCIETY
• Generates ideas for creating images based on a particular theme.	• Uses paint effectively to create a picture. • Creates an image using fingers and knuckles.	• Self-evaluates and discusses own work.	• Expresses thoughts and feelings through art making.

Klimt sleeping portrait

DURATION

Three lessons

TASK

Create a portrait of oneself asleep, based on Gustav Klimt's artwork.

MATERIALS

✓ pictures or photographs of Gustav Klimt's artwork: refer to <http://www.oceansbridge.com/oil-paintings/product/38095/thekiss190708>

✓ cartridge paper   ✓ watercolour paint/edicol dye   ✓ glue

✓ black permanent marker   ✓ brushes   ✓ black card

✓ lead pencils   ✓ water and containers   ✓ gold pen/pencil

✓ erasers   ✓ scissors

LESSON 1

1. Look at and discuss Gustav Klimt's artwork, 'The kiss'. Discuss his use of pattern in the quilts and his use of colour.

2. Demonstrate drawing a side profile portrait and discuss how to draw one to show that the person is asleep.

3. Students then attempt to draw their own profile portrait, using about one-third of the page for the head. The remainder of the page will be the quilt. (These portraits also work well when the students use a full face view.)

4. Draw a pillow shape behind the head and divide the quilt into large 'patchwork' shapes.

5. Inside each shape, use pencil to draw a different pattern. Once the students are happy with the design, trace over it in black permanent marker.

LESSON 2

Use watercolour paint or edicol dye to complete each patchwork section in a different colour. Paint hair, face and pillow in appropriate colours and leave to dry.

LESSON 3

Use gold pen to trace pattern shapes in selected patchwork spaces. Cut around quilt and pillow shape and glue onto black card.

EVALUATION

ARTS IDEAS	ARTS SKILLS AND PROCESSES	ARTS RESPONSES	ARTS IN SOCIETY
• Uses ideas of other artists to inspire own artwork.	• Creates a variety of patterns. • Draws a self-portrait.	• Responds to visual art through making another artwork.	• Looks at Gustav Klimt's artwork and discuss processes and techniques.

Cockatoo

DURATION

Two lessons

TASK

Draw and colour an image of a cockatoo.

MATERIALS

- ✓ pictures or photographs of cockatoos
- ✓ cartridge paper
- ✓ pencils
- ✓ erasers
- ✓ black permanent markers

- ✓ oil pastels
- ✓ blue and green edicol dye
- ✓ brushes
- ✓ water and containers

LESSON 1

1. Look at and discuss pictures or photographs of cockatoos to assist students with their drawings.

2. The students follow guided drawing instructions to draw their own cockatoo, using lead pencil on cartridge paper.

3. Once happy with their drawing, students trace over them in black permanent marker.

4. Use oil pastels to colour the cockatoo and tree branch, ensuring the students press quite hard to get vibrant colour with no gaps.

LESSON 2

Mix blue and green edicol dye to create an aqua/green colour. Paint the background. Allow to dry.

EVALUATION

ARTS IDEAS	ARTS SKILLS AND PROCESSES	ARTS RESPONSES	ARTS IN SOCIETY
• Generates ideas for creating images based on a theme.	• Follows step-by-step instructions to draw an image. • Uses oil pastels effectively to colour an image.	• Self-evaluates and discusses own work.	• Uses photographs to inspire and draw knowledge from.

Yabby

DURATION

Two lessons

TASK

Draw and colour an image of a yabby (freshwater crayfish).

MATERIALS

- ✓ pictures or photographs of yabbies (optional)
- ✓ 2 sheets of cartridge paper (one for the background and one for the yabby)
- ✓ lead pencils
- ✓ erasers
- ✓ dark and light blue oil pastels

- ✓ black permanent markers
- ✓ scissors
- ✓ glue
- ✓ yellow card
- ✓ black/brown edicol dye
- ✓ eye-dropper

LESSON 1

Use brown or black edicol dye to create a spotted background using an eye-dropper on yellow card. Allow to dry. (If yellow card is not available, ask the students to paint a sheet of paper yellow.)

LESSON 2

1. Discuss yabbies and their features. If necessary, show pictures or photographs. Use guided drawing instructions to show the students how to draw a yabby on cartridge paper using lead pencil.

2. Once happy with their drawings, the students trace over them using black permanent marker.
3. Use dark blue oil pastel to colour the outside edges of the yabby's body parts. Use light blue for the middle sections, blending with the dark blue.
4. Carefully cut out the yabby and glue to background.

EVALUATION

ARTS IDEAS	ARTS SKILLS AND PROCESSES	ARTS RESPONSES	ARTS IN SOCIETY
• Generates ideas for creating images based on a theme.	• Follows step-by-step instructions to draw an image. • Uses oil pastels effectively.	• Self-evaluates and discusses own work.	• Expresses thoughts and feelings through art making.

R.I.C. Publications®

Dragonfly

DURATION

Two lessons

TASK

Draw and colour a dragonfly and create a collage of a garden background.

MATERIALS

- ✓ cartridge paper
- ✓ lead pencils
- ✓ erasers
- ✓ black permanent markers
- ✓ water soluble crayons

- ✓ brushes
- ✓ water and containers
- ✓ glue
- ✓ scissors
- ✓ yellow crepe paper

- ✓ coloured cupcake papers
- ✓ blue card
- ✓ green crayons

LESSON 1

1. Use guided drawing instructions to assist students to draw a dragonfly on cartridge paper using lead pencil.

2. Once students are satisfied with their drawing, trace over it in black permanent marker.

3. Use water soluble crayons to colour the dragonfly's body. Use red for the edges and yellow for the middle. When painted with water, the colours will blend to give a colour progression of red-orange-yellow.

4. Use blue and green water soluble crayons to lightly shade the wings. Blend the colours by painting with water. Allow to dry.

LESSON 2

1. Cut out and glue the dragonfly onto blue card.

2. Select about five or six different coloured cupcake papers and cut along the rippled edge, stopping at the beginning of the round base section.

3. Glue the round base of each cupcake paper near the bottom of the blue card and fluff out the cut ends so that the cupcake papers resemble flowers.

4. Tear, scrunch and glue pieces of yellow crepe paper into the middle of each flower. Use green crayon to draw stems for each flower.

EVALUATION

ARTS IDEAS	ARTS SKILLS AND PROCESSES	ARTS RESPONSES	ARTS IN SOCIETY
• Generates ideas for artwork.	• Uses water soluble crayons effectively.	• Self-evaluates and discusses own work.	• Expresses thoughts and feelings through art.

R.I.C. Publications®

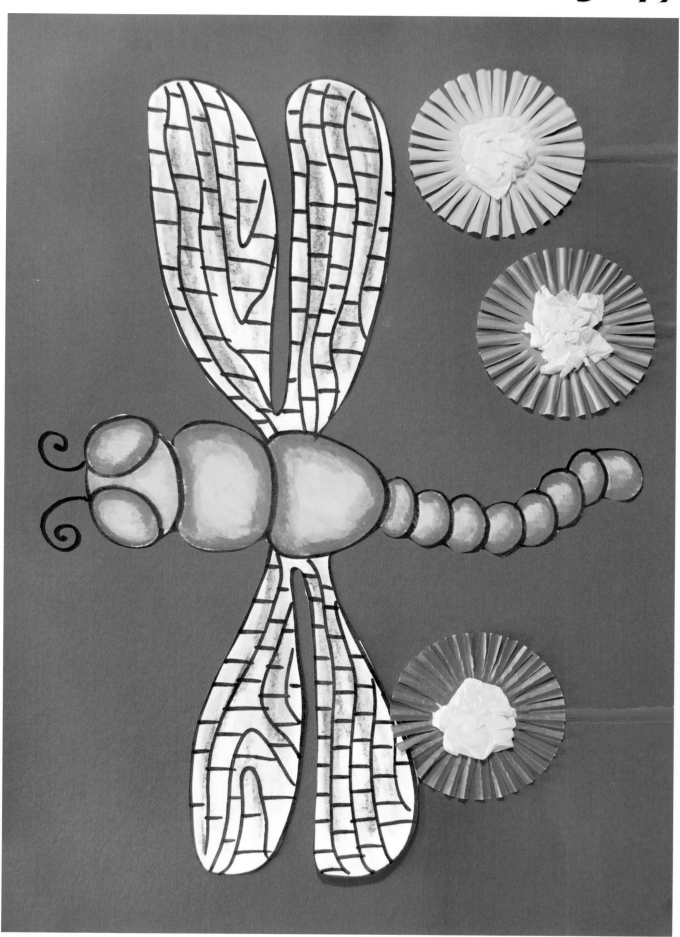

Praying mantis

DURATION

Three lessons

TASK

Draw a praying mantis and create a garden background.

MATERIALS

- ✓ cartridge paper
- ✓ lead pencils
- ✓ erasers
- ✓ black permanent markers
- ✓ green and yellow oil pastels
- ✓ PVA glue
- ✓ bark, leaf fronds etc.
- ✓ brown, green and yellow edicol dye
- ✓ eye-droppers
- ✓ large googly eyes (optional)

LESSON 1

1. Use guided drawing to assist students to draw a praying mantis on the cartridge paper using lead pencil.

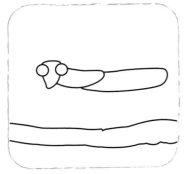  

2. Once the students are happy with their drawings, trace over them with black permanent marker.
3. Use green oil pastel to colour around the edges of the praying mantis' body and yellow for the inside areas. Blend the area where the colours meet to create a yellow/green colour.

LESSON 2

1. Use the eye-dropper to carefully drop brown, green and yellow splotches of edicol dye, in order, around the praying mantis for the background. Allow to dry.

LESSON 3

1. Use PVA glue to glue bark or leaf fronds onto the tree branch.
2. If available, large googly eyes can be glued onto the praying mantis.

EVALUATION

ARTS IDEAS	ARTS SKILLS AND PROCESSES	ARTS RESPONSES	ARTS IN SOCIETY
• Generates ideas for artwork.	• Follows step-by-step instructions. • Uses oil pastels effectively.	• Self-evaluates and discusses own work.	• Expresses thoughts and feelings through art making.

R.I.C. Publications®

Pelican

DURATION

Two lessons

TASK

Draw and colour an image of a pelican.

MATERIALS

- ✓ cartridge paper
- ✓ lead pencils
- ✓ erasers
- ✓ black permanent markers

- ✓ water soluble crayons
- ✓ brushes
- ✓ water and containers

LESSON 1

1. Model drawing a pelican for the students, discussing the size of the beak and other body features.

2. The students then draw their own pelican. Draw a line across the page about one-fifth of the way down. Draw vertical stripes in this section for reeds above the water.

3. Once the students are happy with their drawing, trace over them using black permanent marker.

4. Use water soluble crayons to colour the picture—blue for the water, alternate light and dark green for the reeds and orange and skin colour for the beak. For the pelican's body, colour the edges and any feather lines in black.

LESSON 2

Paint the picture with water. When painting the pelican's body, use quite a lot of water to dissolve the black and colour the pelican a very light grey. Allow to dry.

EVALUATION

ARTS IDEAS	ARTS SKILLS AND PROCESSES	ARTS RESPONSES	ARTS IN SOCIETY
• Generates ideas for creating an artwork.	• Uses water soluble crayons effectively.	• Self-evaluates and discusses own work.	• Expresses thoughts and feelings through making artwork.

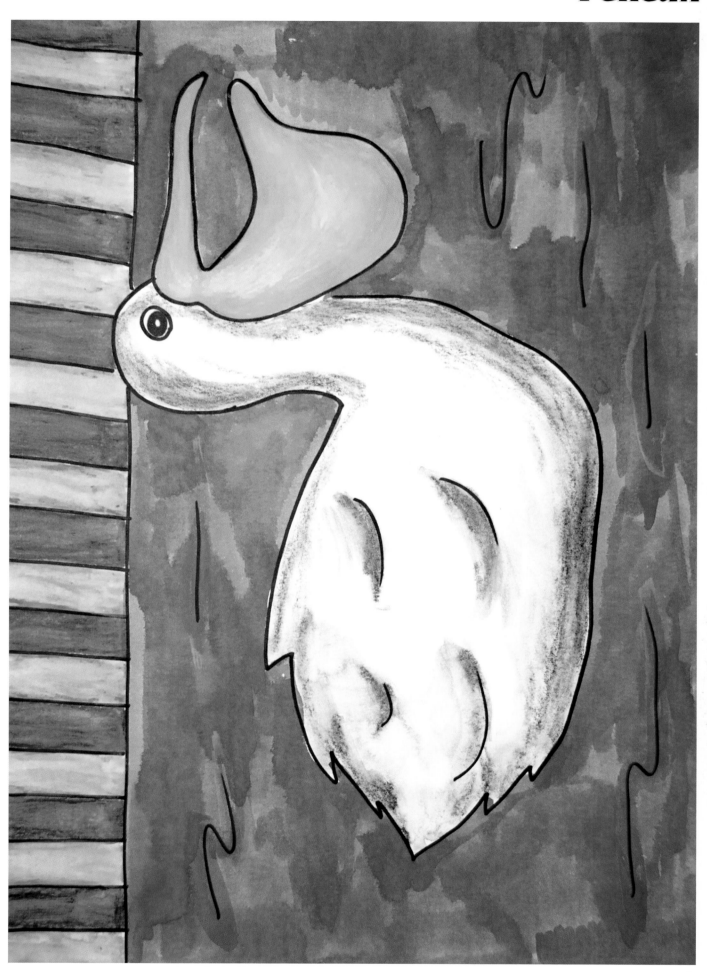

Stegosaurus

DURATION

Two lessons

TASK

Draw a stegosaurus and create a jungle background.

MATERIALS

- ✓ two sheets cartridge paper
- ✓ lead pencils
- ✓ erasers
- ✓ black permanent markers
- ✓ water soluble crayons
- ✓ water and containers
- ✓ brushes

- ✓ scissors
- ✓ glue
- ✓ origami paper
- ✓ green and brown paint
- ✓ sponges (or sponge pieces cut to size)
- ✓ green corrugated card

LESSON 1

1. Sponge paint one sheet of cartridge paper using green and brown paint and leave to dry.

2. Discuss the features of a stegosaurus—large body, long tail, small head. Demonstrate drawing a stegosaurus leaving out the spine plates. Encourage the students to use the entire page when drawing their own version. Students will need to draw a thin oval shape for the ground.

3. Once the students have drawn their own stegosaurus, they trace over it using black permanent marker.

4. Colour the stegosaurus using brown and ochre water soluble crayons and colour the ground green. Paint with water to dissolve pigment and leave to dry.

LESSON 2

1. Cut out and glue stegosaurus onto sponge painted background. Use origami paper to cut out a variety of different sized spine plates. Glue these along the stegosaurus's body, placing the smaller plates near the tail and head and larger ones along the back.

2. Cut leaf shapes from green corrugated card and glue them along the bottom edge of the page.

EVALUATION

ARTS IDEAS	ARTS SKILLS AND PROCESSES	ARTS RESPONSES	ARTS IN SOCIETY
• Generates ideas for creating artwork.	• Draws an image utilising page space. • Cuts and creates a collage of specific shapes.	• Self-evaluates and discusses own work.	• Expresses thoughts and feelings through art making.

R.I.C. Publications®

Birthday cake

DURATION

Two lessons

TASK

Draw a large and colourful birthday cake.

MATERIALS

- ✓ cartridge paper
- ✓ lead pencils
- ✓ erasers
- ✓ black permanent markers

- ✓ oil pastels
- ✓ glue
- ✓ scissors
- ✓ brightly coloured card for background

LESSON 1

1. Discuss different types of cakes, toppings and decorations students have seen or eaten.
2. On cartridge paper, students use the entire page to draw a layered cake, complete with icing and decorations.
3. Draw a plate underneath the cake and decorate with patterns.
4. Trace over all lines using black permanent marker.

LESSON 2

1. Use oil pastels to colour the cake and plate. Encourage the students to use bright colours and press hard when colouring to achieve bold, bright colour with no white gaps.
2. Cut out and glue onto brightly coloured card.

EVALUATION

ARTS IDEAS	ARTS SKILLS AND PROCESSES	ARTS RESPONSES	ARTS IN SOCIETY
• Generate ideas for creating artwork.	• Uses oil pastel effectively.	• Self-evaluates and discusses own work.	• Expresses thoughts and feelings through art making.

www.ricpublications.com.au
R.I.C. Publications®

Christmas pudding

TASK

Create a collage of a Christmas pudding.

MATERIALS

✓ brown and cream coloured paper

✓ scissors

✓ red and green origami paper

✓ glue

✓ Christmas wrapping paper

✓ silver, green and red glitter

✓ lead pencils

✓ erasers

✓ PVA glue in squeeze bottle

✓ red or green card for background

LESSON 1

1. On brown paper, draw a semicircle shape for the cake. Place cream paper underneath and trace the top curved edge then draw a wavy line beneath the curved edge to create the impression of dripping custard. Cut out both pieces.

2. Glue the custard on top of the brown pudding.

3. Draw a long thin oval shape on Christmas wrapping paper to make the plate. Ensure that it is wider than the pudding. Measure roughly if necessary.

4. Glue the plate near the bottom of a sheet of red or green backing card then glue the pudding onto the plate.

5. Using red and green origami paper, draw and cut out three circles for holly berries and leaves to glue on top of the Christmas pudding.

6. Use PVA glue in a squeeze bottle to trace around the edge of the plate. Sprinkle with silver glitter.

7. Trace PVA glue around the holly leaves and berries and sprinkle with red and green glitter. Set aside to dry.

EVALUATION

ARTS IDEAS	ARTS SKILLS AND PROCESSES	ARTS RESPONSES	ARTS IN SOCIETY
• Generates ideas for creating artwork.	• Creates a collage using a variety of materials to create an image.	• Self-evaluates and discusses own work.	• Discusses symbols used in the making of Christmas artwork.

Wavy Christmas tree

DURATION

Two lessons

TASK

Create a Christmas tree collage using paper strips.

MATERIALS

- ✓ wavy Christmas tree worksheet (see page 76)
- ✓ card for photocopying worksheet
- ✓ various shades of green paper
- ✓ origami paper—various colours for the pot, yellow for the star, brown for the tree trunk, various shades of green for strips for the tree.

- ✓ lead pencils
- ✓ glue
- ✓ scissors
- ✓ gold glitter
- ✓ red card for background
- ✓ PVA glue in a squeeze bottle

LESSON 1

1. Provide each student with a photocopy of the wavy Christmas tree worksheet on page 76 on card.
2. Students will need to carefully cut out each section.
3. Trace the pot onto coloured origami paper, the tree trunk onto brown paper and the star onto yellow paper and set aside for later.
4. Cut thin strips of various colours of green paper and glue diagonally across the tree. Once the tree is completely covered in paper strips, turn the tree over and trim any overhanging bits.

LESSON 2

1. Assemble and glue the tree, trunk, pot and star onto red card.
2. Use PVA glue in a squeeze bottle to 'draw' some lines across the tree. Sprinkle gold glitter on the glue lines and allow to dry.

EVALUATION

ARTS IDEAS	ARTS SKILLS AND PROCESSES	ARTS RESPONSES	ARTS IN SOCIETY
• Generates ideas to create an artwork.	• Uses materials to create a collage of an image.	• Self-evaluates and discusses own work.	• Discusses the symbols used in Christmas artwork.

R.I.C. Publications®

Assessment checklist

YEAR 1
DATE 25/02/2010

ART PROJECT

STUDENTS	Makes a drawing of a chameleon using line and shape (AI)	Matches and groups similar colours (ASP)	Responds to photographs by creating another artwork. (AR)	Looks at scientific artwork from the geographic magazines. (AIS)	Uses ideas of other artists to inspire own work. (AI)	Uses chalk pastels effectively to create a specific effect. (ASP)	Responds to visual arts by creating another artwork. (AR)	Looks at Van Gogh's Starry night and other works and discusses painting techniques. (AIS)	Draw various flower parts onto a selection of collage materials. (AI)	Uses a variety of materials to make a collage of an image. (ASP)	Responds to visual arts by making another artwork. (AR)	Looks at Van Gogh's sunflower paintings and discusses the various shades of yellow used. (AIS)
	AI	**ASP**	**AR**	**AIS**	**AI**	**ASP**	**AR**	**AIS**	**AI**	**ASP**	**AR**	**AIS**
	Striped chameleon				Starry night				Sunflowers			
Sam	✔	✔	✔	✔	✔	●	✔	✔	✔	✔	✔	✔
Dayna	✔	✔	✔	✔	✔	✔	✔	✔	✔	✔	✔	✔
Amy	✔	✔	✔	✔	✔	✔	✔	●	✔	✔	✔	●
Shane	✔	✔	✔	✔	✔	✔	✔	✔	✔	✔	✔	✔
Ben	✔	✔	✔	✔	●	●	✔	✔	✔	✔	✔	✔
Layla	✔	✔	✔	✔	✔	✔	✔	✔	✔	✔	✔	✔
Michaela	✔	●	✔	✔	✔	✔	✔	✔	✔	✔	✔	✔
Xin	●	✔	✔	✔	✔	✔	✔	✔	●	●	✔	✔
Abdul	✔	✔	✔	✔	✔	✔	✔	✔	✔	✔	✔	✔
Joseph	✔	●	✔	✔	✔	✔	✔	✔	✔	●	✔	✔
Emma	✔	✔	✔	✔	✔	✔	✔	✔	✔	✔	✔	●
Sophie	✔	✔	✔	✔	✔	✔	✔	✔	✔	●	✔	✔
Max	✔	✔	✔	✔	✔	✔	✔	✔	✔	✔	✔	✔
Xavier	✔	✔	✔	✔	✔	✔	✔	●	✔	✔	✔	✔
Toby	✔	✔	✔	✔	✔	✔	✔	✔	✔	✔	✔	✔
Priya	✔	●	✔	✔	✔	✔	✔	✔	✔	●	✔	✔
Jordan	✔	✔	✔	✔	✔	●	✔	✔	✔	✔	✔	●
Faisal	✔	●	✔	✔	✔	✔	✔	✔	✔	✔	✔	✔
Natasha	✔	✔	✔	✔	✔	✔	✔	✔	✔	✔	✔	✔
Andrew	✔	✔	✔	●	✔	✔	✔	✔	✔	✔	✔	✔

KEY: ✔ demonstrated ● still developing AI—Arts ideas AR—Arts responses ASP—Arts skills and processes AIS—Arts in society

Assessment checklist

YEAR ____

DATE ____

ART PROJECT

	AI	ASP	AR	AIS	AI	ASP	AR	AIS	AI	ASP	AR	AIS
STUDENTS												

KEY: ✔ demonstrated   ● still developing   AI—Arts ideas   AR—Arts responses   ASP—Arts skills and processes   AIS—Arts in society

Student self-assessment sheet

Name: _____ Date: _____

Title of artwork: _____

Materials used: _____

_____

_____

_____

_____

How I created my artwork: _____

_____

_____

_____

_____

The part of the art activity I enjoyed most was: _____

_____

_____

_____

My opinion of the final result: _____

_____

_____

_____

Star rating of my artwork:

Looking at art

Description:

What do you see?

Analysis:

How is the picture or sculpture organised?

colour _____

line _____

texture _____

foreground _____

middle-ground _____

background _____

Interpretation:

What is the artist showing or telling us?

Judgment:

Do you like or dislike the artwork? Why?

Elements of art labels

Different tools make different kinds of **lines**.
Lines can be straight, curved, wavy, thick, thin, long or short. Lines can show size, colour, shape and direction.
Lines can change.

Texture is how the surface of something looks or feels. Texture can be real or implied.

Every **colour** can be bright, dull, dark or light.
Colours can change when mixed together.
Colours can show and make us feel emotion.

Form is three-dimensional and takes up space.

Space exists around us.
We use illusions to make space in art.

Tone refers to darkness and lightness in a painting or drawing.

Shapes come in many types and sizes.
Shapes can change size, colour, texture and pattern.
Shapes can change into symbols.

Enlarge and display these elements of art explanations around the room near artworks that depict each particular element.

Reward ribbons

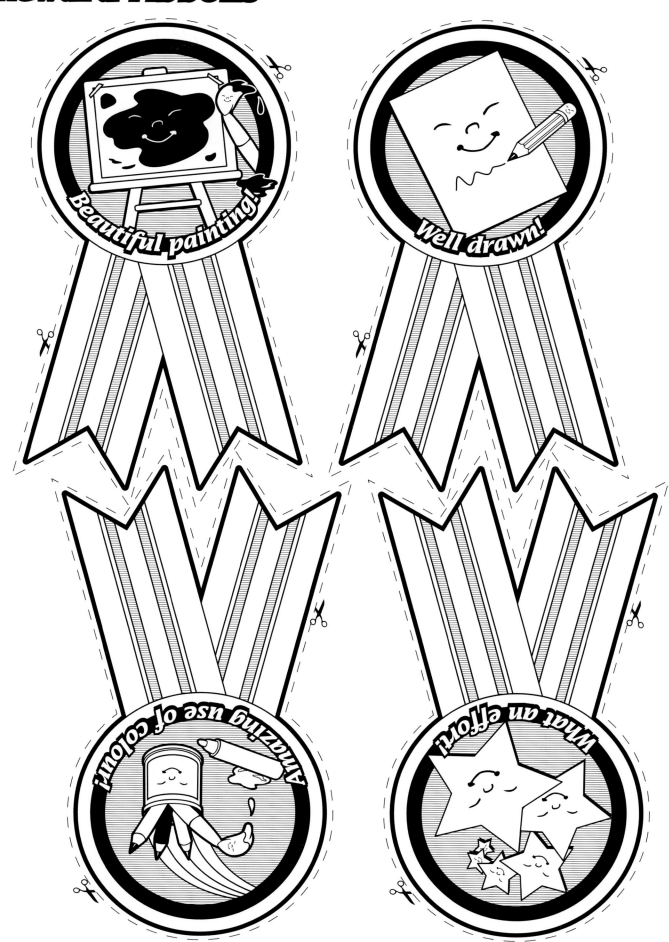

Beautiful painting!

Well drawn!

Amazing use of colour!

What an effort!

Activity card samples—1

Get creative!

Design an alien from outer space.

Use as many patterns as you can to decorate a lizard.

Colour your lizard.

There is no limit to the number of colours you can use!

Activity cards, such as the examples provided, can be completed by the students as 'early finisher' tasks, or as part of their art project.

Activity card samples—2

Photocopy onto card and laminate for durability.

Activity cards, such as the examples provided, can be completed by the students as early finisher tasks, or as part of their art project.

Draw a chameleon and colour it using all the colours of the rainbow!

Remember to use them all: red, orange, yellow, green, blue, indigo, violet.

Create a flower design using patterns.

Colour your design using five colours only.

Build-a-dinosaur – template

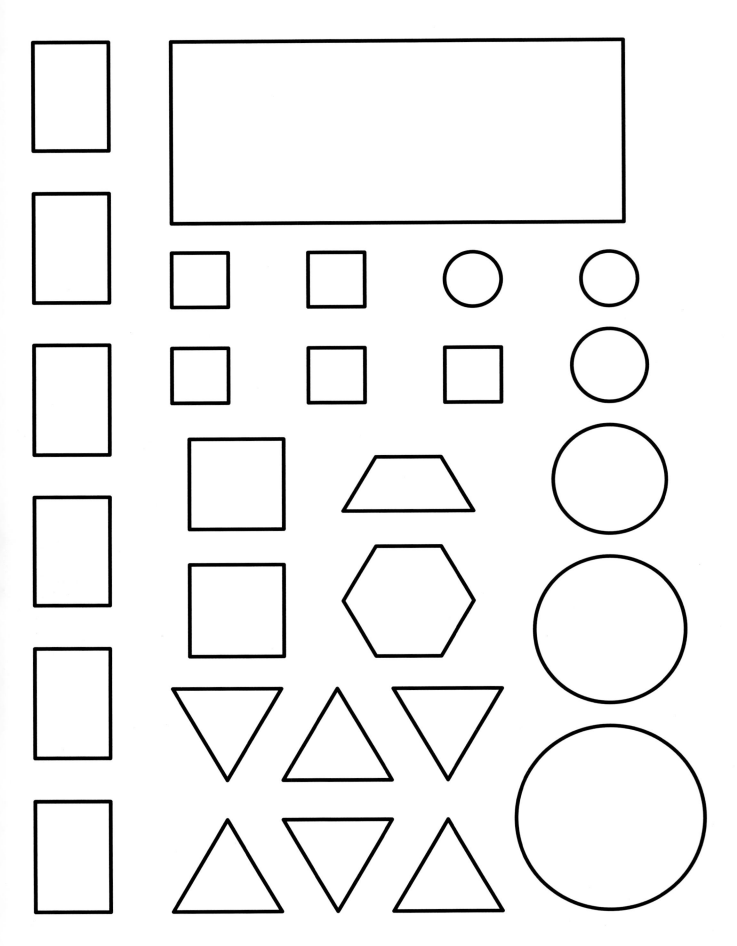

Me and my clothes – template

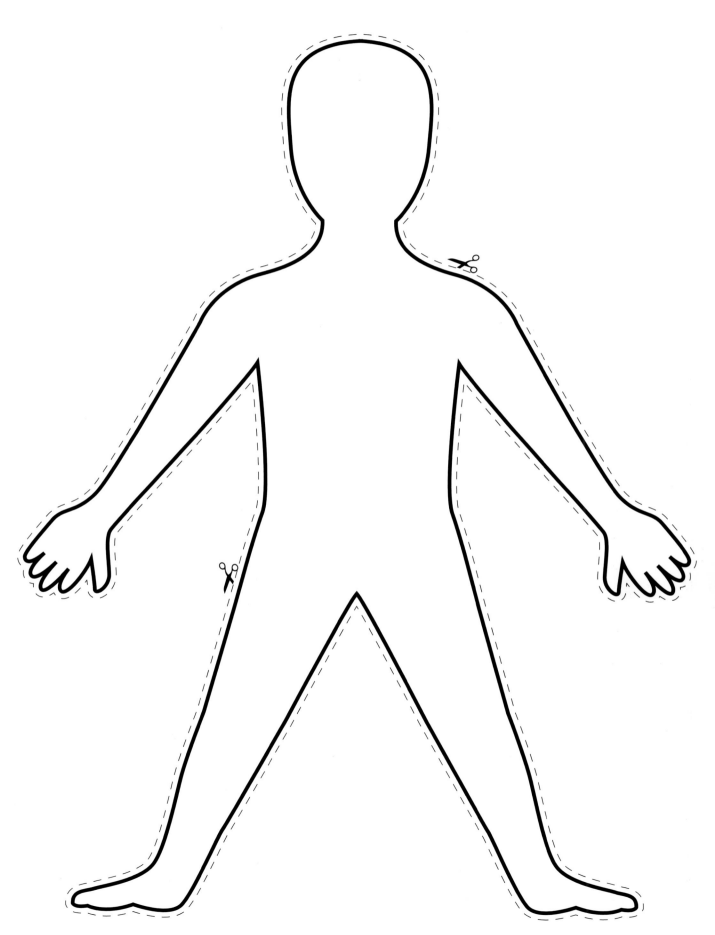

Enlarge to appropriate size if necessary.

Wavy Christmas tree – template

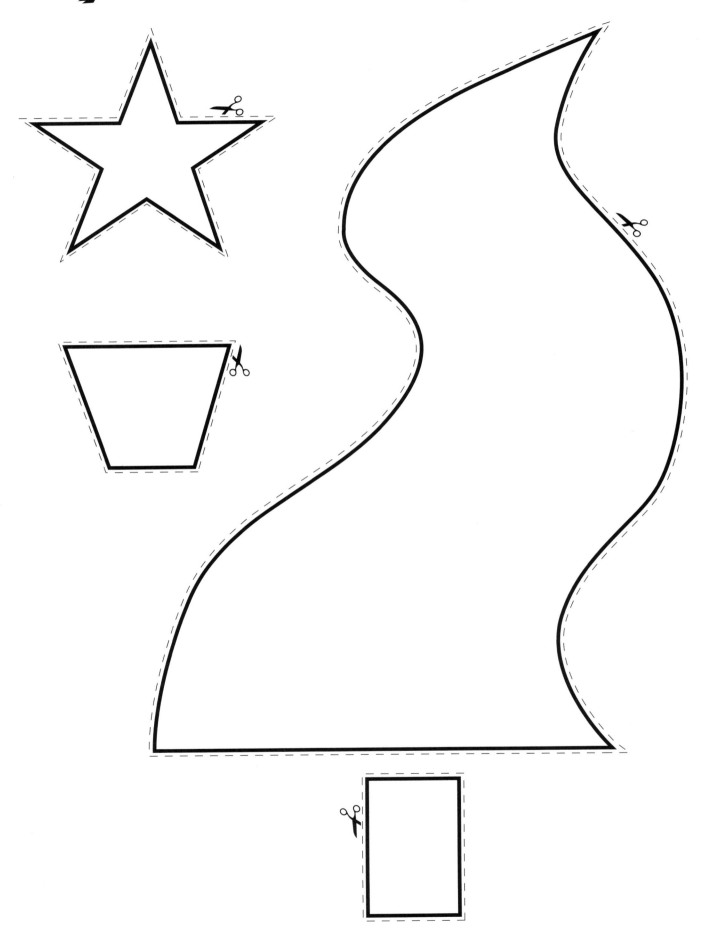

EXPLORING VISUAL ARTS